11.23

11/01

Humdrop

READING POWER

Venus Williams
Tennis Champion
Heather Feldman

The Rosen Publishing Group's
PowerKids Press ™
New York

1

For Sophie Megan

Published in 2001 by The Rosen Publishing Group, Inc.
29 East 21st Street, New York, NY 10010

Copyright © 2001 by The Rosen Publishing Group, Inc.

First Edition

Book Design: Michael de Guzman

Photo Credits: pp. 5, 15, 17, 19 © CLIVE BRUNSKILL/ALLSPORT; p. 7 © KEN LEVINE/ALLSPORT; p. 9 © JACK ATLEY/ALLSPORT; p. 11 © AL BELLO/ALLSPORT; pp. 13, 21 © GARY M. PRIOR/ALLSPORT.

Feldman, Heather.
    Venus Williams / Feldman, Heather [sic].— 1st ed.
        p. cm.— (Reading power)
    Includes index.
    Summary: A biography of the young tennis player who has been ranked among the top ten women players in the world.
    ISBN 0-8239-5717-9 (alk. paper)
    1. Williams, Venus, 1980- —Juvenile literature. 2. Tennis players—United States—Biography—Juvenile literature. 3. Afro-American women tennis players—Biography—Juvenile literature. [1. Williams, Venus, 1980- 2. Tennis players. 3. Afro-Americans—Biography. 4. Women—Biography.] I. Title. II. Series.

GV994.W49 F45 2001
796.342'092—dc21
[B]   00-022494

Manufactured in the United States of America

2

Contents

Venus Williams plays tennis.

Venus has played tennis for many years. She has played since she was a young girl.

7

Venus has a sister named Serena. Serena plays tennis, too.

Venus and Serena win
prizes. They are both
great tennis players.
They are great
friends, too.

11

Venus can move fast. She moves fast to get to the ball.

Venus can jump high. She jumps high to hit the ball.

Venus likes to wear
her hair in beads.
Venus has a lot
of style.

Venus uses a big racket. She uses the racket to hit the tennis ball hard.

Venus is happy when she wins a prize. She wins prizes for playing tennis. Venus is a great tennis player.

21

Glossary

prizes (PRYZ-iz) What a person sometimes gets when he or she wins games.

racket (RAK-it) The object a tennis player holds and uses to hit the tennis ball.

style (STYL) A special way of acting or looking that makes a person who he or she is.

tennis (TEN-is) A sport where two or four people hit a ball back and forth over a net using tennis rackets.

Here is another good book to read about Venus Williams:

Venus Williams (Galaxy of Superstars)
By Virginia Aronson
Chelsea House Publishers

To learn more about tennis, check out these Web sites:
http://www.yahooligans.com/Sports_
    and_Recreation/Tennis
http://www.excite.com/sports/tennis/

To learn more about Venus Williams, check out these Web sites:
http://www.williamssisters.com
http://espn.go.com/editors/ten/
    profiles/williams.html

Index

Word Count: 118

Note to Librarians, Teachers, and Parents

If reading is a challenge, Reading Power is a solution! Reading Power is perfect for readers who want high-interest subject matter at an accessible reading level. These fact-filled, photo-illustrated books are designed for readers who want straightforward vocabulary, engaging topics, and a manageable reading experience. With clear picture/text correspondence, leveled Reading Power books put the reader in charge. Now readers have the power to get the information they want and the skills they need in a user-friendly format.